TWO PLAYS OF

WAR AND PEACE

Plays by Rodney Quinn:

Over The Top

Birds Still Fly

See Emily Not Play

A Cleaner Point of View

Capture The Flag

Doug and Lillian

Jerome Connor

My Friend Al

Burgundy

TWO PLAYS OF
WAR AND PEACE

Birds Still Fly

Over The Top

Rodney Quinn

First published in Great Britain by Amaurea Press 2025
Amaurea Press is an imprint of Amaurea Creative Productions Ltd.
www.amaureapress.com

Copyright © Rodney Quinn 2025

The right of Rodney Quinn to be identified as the author of this work has been asserted in accordance with the Copyright, Designs and Patents Act 1988

All rights reserved. Apart from any fair dealing for the purposes of criticism or review, as permitted under the Copyright Acts, no part of this book may be reproduced, copied or transmitted in any form or by any electronic or mechanical means, including information storage and retrieval systems, without permission in writing from the publisher.

ISBN 978-1-914278-72-3 (paperback)
ISBN 978-1-914278-74-7 (eBook)

British Library Catalogue in Publishing Data
A catalogue record for this book is available from the British Library.

Book design and typesetting by Albarrojo
Cover design by Rodney Quinn and Albarrojo, based on original artwork by Chris Greene

For my daughter

Martha Quinn

and my mother

Anne

Contents

Introduction

9

Birds Still Fly

13

Over The Top

55

Introduction

I first met Rodney backstage at the South London Theatre, as I was just embarking on my own short-lived acting career. As I recall, it was a production of Tom Stoppard's *Rosencrantz and Guildenstern are Dead*. I had a very minor part, which barely warranted a credit, and so there was a lot of hanging around waiting for a brief moment in the limelight. Rodney was an assistant stage manager, and I forget how we began to talk – but as soon as we did, we found that we understood one another.

It was the beginning of a beautiful friendship. A few months later, Rodney was casting for a production of his two war plays, *Over The Top* and *Birds Still Fly* – and he surprised me by casting me in the latter. His call came just as I was on my way to another audition, which his offer more than trumped.

The role of Hackett came at just the right moment for me. A character I could pour my nascent thespian impulses into. The wooden owl I portrayed Hackett as carving in the midst of his battlefield quest to find his son still sits proudly on my shelf. And Rodney never fails to tease me about it.

Since then, Rodney and I have continued to collaborate on creative projects. Attempting to kickstart independent cultural ventures and writing projects together. Improvised happenings in Deptford. A First World War play (*Capture The Flag*), which as well as having a London fringe run, ended up being toured to schools and prisons. A monologue performance of his *Burgundy*. Acting and theatre groups, bringing together fellow restless spirits. Countless ideas for films that have yet to be made. And the sharing of life's trials and tribulations – of which Rodney has had far more than his fair share.

Rodney was born in Dublin, and grew up in Greystones, County Wicklow. After his mother left for London with Rodney's two siblings, he was left alone with his father. But eventually she came back for him, and his later teenage years were spent in the English capital.

From early on, Rodney travelled around a lot. Backwards and forwards to Ireland: Galway, and later Cork. A Buddhist group in Leicester. Glasgow. Yorkshire. His restlessness has not stopped since. Nor has his ability to strike up conversations with the most unlikely of strangers. Unable to resist cracking a joke, or making an irreverent comment. Collecting in the process the experiences and the human interactions that he channels into his writing.

Rodney started writing in the early 1990s when living in Cork. Being dyslexic and not able to spell, he began messing around with wordplay poems. He didn't start writing plays until 2004, when he was involved with the Cork Arts Theatre. It was there that he wrote *Over The Top* and *Birds Still Fly* – his first plays, and though he went on to write several others, these are the two that have been most performed.

He has been writing ever since, channelling his own demons – and those he can discern in those he encounters – into an ability to turn the darkest of situations into an amusing one.

JONATHAN CURRY-MACHADO

I think there's an anger in these two plays. It's kind of an anti-rich thing. They're kind of socialist plays about the rich controlling the poor, making the poor do their dirty work for them, in the disguise of honouring your country and all that.

Rodney Quinn

BIRDS STILL FLY

Rodney Quinn

Birds Still Fly came of an epic poem that I wrote. I was having a few pints watching a football match. I don't remember who was playing, but a bird flew across like in a dream. You don't normally see that. It was a seagull. And I thought: 'Birds, they still fly.' And I thought, 'That sounds like an epic anti-war poem.' And so I wrote it.

I suppose it just came naturally that I would set it in the Crusades. I felt that it had to be done with weird dialogue. It just came out that way.

I find that if you find the characters in your head and you give them names, then they kind of write their own story. If you know who they are, and how they feel about a situation, and how they reply to another person's statement, I think it writes itself.

RODNEY QUINN

First performed as *Birds They Still Fly*, February 2007,
Cork Arts Theatre, Cork City, Ireland

Mother: Suzy Campbell
Hackett: Paul Casey
Abelard: Aidan O'Shea
Gifford: Colin Patrick Kelleher

Birds Still Fly performed March 2013
South London Theatre, London
Directed by Chaz Doyle and Rodney Quinn

Eda: Kelly-Kim Cranstoun
Hackett: Jonathan Curry
Abelard: Chaz Doyle
Gifford: Peter Bond
Ulric: Jake Passmore

Characters

Eda: A grieving mother

Hackett: A grieving father

Abelard: Captain of the King's Army

Gifford: A Soldier

Ulric: The ghost of Hackett's son

Prologue (optional)

*Enter **Eda***

Eda
> Eda is my name, but to most I am Mother. Neither name have I heard this past two months. It has not been just lonely, but a time of bitter worries and fears it has been. Fear for my kin! For I, mother without son first, and then without husband. My beloved son Ulric taken to war in a far off land, and he not yet reached his fifteenth year. I thought for a week that he was not twenty miles from here, working on my very own cousin's farm, but what I heard was that on his way there, these men of the King's army shined gold coins in his eyes and spoke about the fight for the glory of God, and his young heart was sold. And to the Holy Land he went.
>
> My dear husband, Hackett, beloved father to Ulric, not wanting to lose our son to this madness, has followed the army's path to the Holy Land, to bring him home to me. Two months my beloved Hacket gone, my son, I have not seen him for two months and fortnight this night. And I feel fear and I was not to feel so. I may not see him again, and the worst be I may never see both again. No longer a mother. No more love will I receive in this cold world. I will live broken.

Night near a battlefield in a far-off land. **Hackett** *is mourning over the grave of his son* **Ulric**.

Hackett
Ulric, why did you not listen to your father! Set your eyes upon glory and gold. In the name of God these men sold this falsehood. This be sin, this be hell, this be murder, not glory nor gold but greed. They are foolish men who have no care for the living if they but stand upon their path to gold. In the name of God they kill.

Silence. **Abelard** *enters carrying his sword on his shoulder and a vessel of wine. He looks at* **Hackett** *as he mourns.*

Abelard
So, you are the father of this brave man who lies not half a day under this soil. He fought a fight like a man of God and died like a saint right by my side.

Hackett
I am Hackett, a father without a son, who are you sir!

Abelard
I am Sir Abelard, Knight to our King and servant of our Lord above.

Hackett
I hear what they say of you, sir. They say you are Brave Abelard, they say you killed a hundred men this day.

Abelard
I do not hide from the name Brave Abelard as I do not hide from these dogs that call themselves holy, for they could not be holy like our men, who fight and die in the name of our Lord above, God of all you see.

Hackett
Our Lord above must be proud of you, Brave Abelard, that you will kill for Him, so many of His mankind. You kill in His name. How brave of you.

Abelard
I fight not our Lord's men. I spill the blood of these dogs, the devil kin. Not a hundred a day, as the brave men of our army speak, no sir. It may be twenty, it may be thirty, if the mongrels, women and young be counted.

Hackett
His women and young, how brave you are, sir. But are we not all the Lord's children, Brave Abelard?

Abelard
No, we are not all His children. These dogs are the kin of Lucifer. Soon the day will come when his kin will not walk this earth.

Hackett
Kin of the devil, you say?

Abelard
Yes! Free ourselves, of them, we must. Soon that day will come.

Hackett
It be God's test for us and we have lost. God above does not want men to kill each other. He wants us to live in harmony, for we are all God's kin. We hurt our Lord with these wars.

Abelard
Hurt! No, we serve him until that day will come when we have cleansed these lands for Him.

Hackett
I will cry a tear for mankind and its blindness, for that day, like this, will be another dark day and an end to all days.

Abelard
What strange words you speak. Words of sorrow I feel. But not a dark day, no sir, that day will be a day of light. Now come speak no more of these dogs. You need rest, you have mourned enough for your son. A long way you have travelled. Come, eat! Gifford! Somebody fetch me Gifford! Your son was a friend of God and so you be a friend of mine. On the morrow we go to battle, to fight this foe that brought your kin to death, and for king and God we will spill the blood of the devil's servants across this land.

Hackett
Brave Abelard, late be this day, that I have mourned and cast my shadow over the broken body of my own flesh and blood. Not a long hour be he under the soil and of battle you speak. Why are your words cold as this night air?

Why do you not stand by my side an hour to mourn sweet Ulric? Was he not a fellow countryman, did he not do his duty for God, or was he only to you a poor man's son? Come, ponder upon this grave, what battle has done to my kin and the kin of many a father and mother.

Gifford enters.

Gifford
Yes, Sir Abelard.

Abelard
Gifford, fetch some food for this mourning father and I!

Gifford
Yes, Sir Abelard.

Gifford leaves.

Abelard
I feel your sorrow, Hackett! You were a good father to dear brave Ulric. Your son fought for God, as you will! Ulric no longer walks this ground. His soul will stand beside us for he knows, that many will be no more if men stand and cry for the fallen of yesterday.

Hackett
You cannot feel my sorrow, sir, as I cannot feel yours if you have sorrow.

Gifford enters with a pot and bag on his back and stands watching the two men.

Abelard
> Turn your sorrow into rage. Take arms this morn for God, our King and Ulric, for this will bring us many morrows of freedom . . . Food, man!

Gifford hands Abelard a plate and a spoon and start giving him the food.

Gifford
> This be good food, Sir Abelard.

Gifford stands watching the two men.

Abelard
> Do not just stand there, man! Feed good Hackett. Come now, stop your mourning and eat this hearty meal that Gifford has made this night and sleep strong. Now rest your sleepless body on his grave, one last night will you have by his side.

Abelard sits down and eats his food and drinks wine at some distance from Hackett. Gifford hands Hackett a plate and a spoon and starts giving him the food.

Gifford
> Here, good sir, eat. This be fresh. There be meat, and it be cow not horse, for our jaws are broken from the chewing of old plough horses. It be soft. Eat, sir!

Hackett
> I thank you, good Gifford. Please tell me, did you meet my son?

Hackett starts eating the food.

Gifford
Yes, I did. He was a merry young man. I have seen many a bright boy, in battle die, for that be the life we lead. Your son, he was a good man. I mourn with you, Hackett.

Hackett
Did he fight like a man? Brave Abelard has told me so.

Gifford
Sir Abelard has mind that bends the truth.

Hackett
Tell me more, Gifford.

Gifford
He fought brave, sir. But he fought like a boy. Sir Abelard has bent you a lie. He could not tell you that Ulric was young for battle, for he believes in victory. If he had to fight with an army of boys and girls no older than ten years, then he would, for he fights for England and God.

Hackett
It be not for our land, nor for God that he fights, but for he himself.

Gifford
No! He fights for God, sir. It be sad to kill, but our Lord wishes for his christians to be triumphal. For we are His people.

Hackett
We are all God's people, good Gifford. No person should

die in his name. For those who kill and die in his name are fools. My son was a fool, but he was young and he did not know the evil that men do. Can you not see this!

Abelard *(Shouting)*
More food man!

Gifford
(To Abelard) I come sir! *(To Hackett)* Ulric was no fool. He believed as I do that what he was doing was for our Lord above! And he came to his death with that belief. But he be safe now, sir. He be in peace.

Abelard
More food man! Stop your talking and bring me more while there be still heat in it.

Hackett
You are a fool. Not like my son, because you're a man of age. Can you not see that you do not fight for God, but for the greed of rich men?

Gifford
(To Abelard) I come sir! *(To Hackett)* If I do not believe their words, I have nothing, and then I be dead.

Abelard
God, man! I will not ask again. Bring me that food!

Hackett
Your master calls. Go to him, for you are a free man.

Gifford gives him a strange look.

Gifford
Forgive me, Sir Abelard, I comfort sad Hackett. Good sir, here be the food, sir, there still be heat in it.

*He starts giving **Abelard** the food.*

Abelard
There be work to do this night. Do not spend your hour with this man, for he mourns too long. I mourn our fallen men at the day's end, with our Lord's prayer. An hour! The time I give to mourn, then I move my thinking to the living and to keeping them alive. More men to fight the next battle be the greater good. Keeping our army strong, for that be God's will.

Gifford
And his will it be, for it be the only one we have, Brave Abelard.

Abelard
There be only one God, so there be only one will, and it be ours, for the more we take of this world the better it be for this world.

Gifford
And the better it be for all the people.

Abelard
Yes, in time it will be a land of only rich people, for God will reward his kin for all the good we do on this field of battle.

Gifford
That day I wish to see.

Abelard
First this day! And this day needs more wine. I am out! Fetch me more.

Gifford
Yes! Brave Abelard, I not a moment will I be gone.

Gifford leaves

Abelard *(Shouting)*
Two vessels, man! For I need a strong sleep this night. Hackett, you will need a strong sleep, for we will fight this battle together this morn and many a morrow to come.

Hackett
For who has tomorrows if we die, no more morrows shall be ours.

Abelard
If God will it, that my death be this morn, from the hand of the devil's foe, God's work it will be. For our Lord I will take many a foe with me to my shallow grave. I will fall not alone!

Hackett
Shallow grave will you lay in this day or one to come. For barrels of the blood of men, women and young have you spilt. I see God! And you! Share a glass of wine! With smiles and praise for you, he will make you lord of his heavenly armies. *(He laughs.)* Good sir, I jest! God will be pleased when you sleep in your shallow grave, for less of the blood of man will spill.

Abelard moves very close to **Hackett**.

Abelard
Jest at my death! I will forgive you sir. For you mourn a brave man. But hear my words! This foe if't beat our army on this field of battle I wish it not. But if that come to pass, travel they will, killing all God's people that stand upon their path! Our home will burn! Murder! Without a Mercy! Young to old. This deed they will do.

Hackett
Eye for an eye! If that did take them to our land then that be all, not for gold, like our army in this land.

Abelard
Many a foe's blood I spill this day. A family will live many morrows.

Hackett
For every man you killed this day, did you not kill a father or a son?

Abelard
There are no fathers, there are no sons, there be only foe.

Hackett
What are we! Are we not father or son? Are we not foe to them? They are we and we are they, we are one! Same blood. Your men be farmers killing farmers. For God you say, I say gold, gold for a King and his lords.

Abelard
What madness you speak! We are they and they are we!? No! Fight the devil's army we do for God. If riches come upon our path, so be it, they are the people's riches.

Gifford returns with the wine.

Gifford
Here be more wine, sir.

Abelard
Good Gifford! I need it! To help me drown this man's words of madness.

Hackett
Madness be this battle. This be no battle. This be invasion for gold. Madness be this boy, dead beneath this fresh broken earth not yet become his fifteenth year. Glory and gold ware sold to his eyes wrapped with a ribbon of God's words. To kill! I say it be man-made words in our Lord's name. To kill other men and take their land for gold, for a king! How we take God's words and sell to a boy. Wrong be this. I say the word be greed. Gold not God.

Abelard
Madness be this talk. Your son be dead, and that be sad, he was one of many that did die this day. More will die tomorrow. That does not change my will to fight, or good Gifford here.

Gifford
I fight this morn, for God and King.

Hackett
Good Gifford, you are just a fool. But you, sir, have killed too many men. Your true path be flooded with blood. You walk a path of hate when you should walk a path of worship for the living.

Abelard
You need some wine, Hackett. I need some wine! Your words are lost. Gifford's words be more found than yours.

Abelard drinks from a vessel of wine.

Hackett
He fights not for his own will but the will of lords. For if he not fight, he would be hung for treason!

Abelard
Drink! Your words are lost, and you are lost. A little wine might find you again. Gifford fights for God because he be a free man and it be his choice.

Hackett
If I were lost I wish not to be found by you. This man has no choice for he be poor and the poor live at the will of the rich.

Abelard
What do you say, Gifford, do you fight for the rich?

Gifford
No sir!

Abelard
A free man who has a choice. Good Gifford more wine, man!

Gifford
Yes, sir.

Hackett
He has as much choice as that donkey I just ate!

Abelard
This man and every man in this army are free men. They stay and fight for God. Gifford, speak! Tell him you fight in this battle as free man.

Gifford
I fight as free man for Sir Abelard, Hackett.

Hackett
If Sir Abelard were to say Gifford, you may leave for home, would you still stay and fight?

Abelard
Gifford tell him you would stay and die if need be.

Gifford
I believe we fight for God's will, but to leave this battle and make for home would be a great gift, sir.

Hackett
Every man would leave for home this morn and walk away from war if they had that choice.

Abelard
You would leave this morn with Hackett, while these dogs still live on God's land, our land?

Gifford
I would. I am but one and I be more a cook then a fighter, sir. And I do miss my home ever so much, sir.

Hackett
Come with me, Gifford, this morn. You are a free man

and these men he fights have done no wrong to you or your family.

*Abelard picks up his sword and puts it on **Gifford**'s neck.*

Abelard
You walk from this battle, Gifford, and I'll see you hang. I will cut you down this moment if you speak more of this treason.

Gifford
Treason! I mean not to speak so. He makes me think of my home, sir.

*Hackett picks up his sword and puts it on **Abelard**'s neck.*

Hackett
If you have to cut a man down make it one that holds a sword and can give you a fight.

Abelard
Do not add actions to your words. I will not harm this man. Put down your sword and I will mine.

Hackett
You drew yours first, sir, so I believe it be your turn to move.

*Abelard takes his sword away from **Gifford**'s neck. **Hackett** takes his sword away from **Abelard**'s neck.*

Abelard
Go, man, and finish your work, for we have a battle to fight. Speak not of Hackett here, to my men.

Gifford
Yes, Sir Abelard.

Gifford leaves.

Hackett
There goes no free man! There goes a poor man, that lives at your will.

*Abelard picks up is sword and puts it on **Hackett**'s neck.*

Abelard
The next time you draw your sword upon me you best kill me, for I will not be made look weak to my men.

Hackett
I hope there will not be a next time.

Abelard
The next time will be mine, if you speak those words to my men. These men that fight for me have been paid in gold. When we have crushed these dogs they will return to their home rich men. God will reward them kindly also.

Hackett
Dead most will be. The only men who become richer from this foolish war are the ones who already have too much. God will not reward any men for the killing and invasion of this land and its people. They have lived a peaceful life. They did not want this war.

Abelard
This very day, the Sabbath, they attacked and killed God's men. Dogs they are.

Hackett
The swords of your army spilled the first blood when you marched onto their lands.

Abelard
This be not their land, this be the Holy Land, given to us by God. We are His people . . . Come, fight this battle to avenge your son's death. A brave death had he! If you were half as brave a man as your son, whole families would you save. Fight and his young death will not be a loss. Victorious we will be.

Hackett
A loss you speak! Ulric's death be a loss, but one of many that has gone in these days of battle, with many to come. But true lost be these young lives we throw into the pit of hell. This be only a king's greed and lord's glory that these good men die for. And that, brave sir, be nothing!

Abelard
You speak treason!

Hackett
I speak reason! But none there be.

Abelard
Treason! With your words you build walls not even a strong army could climb. Speak not this treason, utter not words of King's greed. Build friendship. Or my sword will speak an end to your treason.

Hackett
Are we not men? Can we not speak under open sky of

what sorrow that beats in our heart by this grave of my good son? And you say he was a brave fighter.

Abelard
Sorrow I see within you. You say true words, but do not make a plague of words. That softens our army's hearts, makes them run to their mothers' arms, not fight like men of God. Against this foe we fight this morn. If you make one man run, you will hang over brave Ulric's body. True words I speak.

Hackett
True words you speak? True words I speak. I will not make a plague of words, sir, but this battle for land, for gold! God! So say you, I say not. I say this killing be plague! That shining greed of plague that blackens man's heart. Gold you get, the King gets! To England comes this gold. The poor see it not. What we see be taxes, sir! The poor farm the land, till hands bleed, then these lords take the profit. We have no land! We fight for nothing! We are without a face! Bones and flesh are we! Meaning nothing to king and lords. Gold they have in their castles, and they fat and warm in cold winter months. For they do not want their people rich. Were we to become rich, sir, who will farm their land? Who will do the hard work for little payment? Who will fight their bloody wars? They keep their people poor to keep them rich. I will not fight this battle. This be a rich man's battle. You can think my words speak treason, I speak freedom.

Abelard
Treason are your words! I would have made you friend. Stood side by side with you in battle. I think you are more foe then friend, Hackett.

Hackett

That be what be! Leave me to mourn Ulric till dark become light, I speak not to your men. No plague of words will pass my lips.

Abelard

Speak not to my men. If you speak even good morrow then your lips have spoken your death. Speak to Ulric till morn, but he will not listen to treason. His eyes look down upon you! His brave soul stands above you! He will cry upon you from the sky. It makes him sorrowful that his father has gone mad and become a coward and will not avenge his death, nor will he fight for God, nor will he fight for his people.

Hackett

If he cry, sir, he cry for those who die this morn, for he know that this be not a fight for God nor the people, our land. If you give me a true battle I will fight, till no arms left to swing my sword, no legs to charge upon foe. This be not a true or good fight. Ulric know it too.

Abelard

I go to rest. I have a foe to fight this morn. I die if I must, for God and King! I will stand no more and listen to these words of madness and treason.

Ablelard goes off, **Hackett** *sits down.* **Gifford** *enters from the other side.*

Gifford

I be but a donkey to these men, to fetch and carry. Foul words like dirt spat at I, like I be dumb animal. There be dogs that live like kings. I live like a dog that belongs to beggar. When I be no more, will my flesh be cut into lumps like an old plough horse and boiled up for stew to feed this hungry army. If that be my path to be the meal, this be my food . . .

Gifford starts playing on a mandolin (for a minute) then he walks off playing it. Ablelard enters (he has taken off his mail). Hackett is sitting down.

Abelard
Your name I will no more say! When I turn my back, you no longer be man to me but a dog of the foe. This dog I will let free. By morn light, be gone dog! For I will kill you! Be gone by morn song! Gifford come here!

Hackett looks at Abelard for a moment without speaking.

Hackett
Birds still fly. They will die like many a man this morn, and like them have no reason to fight, no reason for war. They just wish to live their life under this burning light as we do. So for now, birds still fly, and you will no longer speak my name. One day there will be no birds flying in the sky or creatures on this earth, for man will kill them all with his wars. Wherever you may be, you will see what a waste of all life, and what a waste man has made of this beautiful earth. Then you will think and say my name. Hackett! His words spoke true.

Gifford enters.

Abelard
That be a long day that you wait. I bid you think your words of treason. If we lose this battle, this foe will come

to England. True words I speak. You will fight then as they burn your town and kill your kin.

Silence.

Abelard
Gifford, have you readied my bed!

Gifford
I have, Sir Abelard!

Abelard
Stay a watch over this dog! You have my command to kill him if he speaks to my men. If he be not gone by dawn light, kill him! If I see him here when I arise then you and he will hang on that tree together as free men.

Gifford
I am a cook, sir, I cannot kill a man who mourns his son in cold blood.

Abelard
His day of mourning will be over. Do this and you will live to cook the night's meal. Speak no more to me. I bid you night.

Hackett
I bid a goodnight, Brave Abelard.

Abelard moves away as if to leave, but stops and ponders on his meeting with Hackett.

Abelard
Sorrow be in his heart. Sorrow be in the heart of many a man this day. There be no treason in these men, as there

be in this man. Ulric, his son, was a brave boy. Young was he, his heart beat with rage, fought like a lion for one so young, for he was a rose bud, not yet a flower. Plucked was he from his mother's arms like a rose from a bush. Not yet in blossom, but blossom did he, on this field of battle, till this day took him, by weeds. These weeds I will pull out of this earth, with my sword or be it with bare hands. I will this morn, a bloody morn be it, for life without war, be life without water, or without wine! We be dry like stone, what be stone? Nothing it be! War gives reason to life, gives gold, land to farm, food to table. It be not pretty painting like the finest art from the finest artist, but every painting has its tale. The tales war brings, they be bloody, but needed. War brings gold, with gold we buy land and with land comes work. With work comes food, good life, and with good life good, strong and many young. With many young, we need more food, more land, more we build, so more gold we need, then we need to fight once again! With this life we need war as we need water. And not forget the wine! If war not happen for many a year, this fool will see! When he begs in the dirt for bread, he will kill his neighbour for crumbs. We close door on war, man will open, for that be the way of man. I have talked too much this day. Rest I must!

*Abelard leaves. **Gifford** is standing away from **Hackett** to his right, who gets up from the grave and comes a little closer to him.*

Hackett

Gifford, you will kill this morn?

Gifford

I have no wish to do this act, sir. I beg you heed Sir Abelard's words, good Hackett.

Hackett
Without my dear Ulric, my life be a blank page on which no words shall be writ. Soon I lie beside him in shallow grave of my own, by the sword of Gifford or maybe Sir Abelard. My sin will be to save many a life that be marked with death, in this bloody battle to come. A lie I have made to Abelard, for a plague of words will I spread this night before light comes! If I can but get one man to turn his back on this battle, I will save many that could die by his sword. That will be worth my life. Now Ulric my son, I must speak a plague of worship of life, the life of all creatures of this beautiful earth. Many I will save. I bid you are at rest. Soon I will be by your side.

Gifford
I cannot let you do this. You be a foolish man.

Hackett
Help me save some of these men from death in this fruitless battle and before light comes, I will help you on your journey home.

Gifford
I cannot help you, I cannot run sir, I will be a hunted man. Go back and mourn your son, sir, and before light comes I will walk you to the foot of the hill.

Hackett
You are a fool, Gifford, and you will die a slave.

Gifford
That be my choice.

Hackett walks back to Ulric's grave and bows his head over the grave. He picks up a rock.

Hackett
You have a choice and so do I, and mine will be words of freedom.

Ulric appears.

Ulric
Father!

Hackett
*(To **Gifford**)* Why do you call me father?

Gifford
I did not call you father, for I did not speak!

Ulric
No, father, it be I.

Hackett
*(To **Gifford**)* Do not jest with me man!

Gifford
I do not jest with you, sir!

***Gifford** moves further away from **Hackett**, and sits down.*

Ulric
No, father, it be I, Ulric! Raise your eyes above.

Hackett
Ulric, it cannot be. How do you stand here beside me? It's

not an hour gone, that I put you under this soil. Come and hold your Father.

Ulric
No, father, your Ulric that walked this earth with you for many a year, his body lies beneath that soil. I am his soul come back to say my goodbyes, and ease your sorrow that you feel.

Gifford closes his eyes and falls asleep.

Hackett
Sorrow your words make me so, but my heart warms to see you one last time with my eyes and to hear your voice with my ears.

Ulric
That pleases me! Father!

Hackett
Father, you say! That makes my heart fill with tears, my dear son! My Ulric!

Ulric
I spilled blood of men in my short fortnight of battle. I am not proud.

Hackett
Son! You have done wrong! But men like Sir Abelard with their manmade words spoken to you like a gift to a child, these words a gift from God they said, glory and gold for the Lord above. But this gift be empty and their words be empty, for these men seek riches for themselves, for they are evil men.

Ulric

Your words speak the truth. I was sold glory and gold in God's name. A fool I was to listen to these men of greed. Please forgive me father.

Hackett

I forgive you, my beloved son.

Ulric

Father, you are a good man. Do not throw away your life, for you can do plenty of good for all life for many a year to come. Without me your life be not a blank page, and will not be an empty life. You can write words upon many pages. Your words be peace and love and worship for all the living! You will speak, you will write, you will stop many a man going to war. Your words will travel. Do not rush to be by my side in this shallow grave.

Hackett

You speak of morrows that will not come for many a man this morn. But I am here this day, and life will I save this morn. Only Gifford stands in my path.

Ulric

Father, this be waste! You may save one life this night or a hundred, or you may save none! You will still die! And for what. Do not be a fool, father, for you are a wise man. What of Gifford? He is to be marked with death if you do this act. Would you have his blood on your hands?

Hackett

I will save him, as I will save many.

Ulric

You will not save a man this night, you will get yourself and Gifford killed with this foolishness.

Hackett

But I must try. If I do not my life be but a waste. I could save hundred men this night! That be a lot of life to save.

Ulric

If you save a hundred or maybe only five, for that be a lot. That be nothing, to what you could save in many years, if you walk the world. When you speak peace not war, your words will teach and your teaching will go on longer than your life. I speak hundreds and hundreds, or it could be more than that. Ponder these words, father.

Hackett

Your words make me think, but I have nothing to live for, now that you have gone from me. But to save life this night, will make my last hour feel like better times have returned.

Ulric

Mother! Be her not worth living for? She be alone without husband, without son, who died and both left her to live out her life alone. Yes, father you have someone to live for. And you could save many a life.

Hackett

Your mother, my beloved Eda, how could I have forgotten her so. How wrong of me! Yes, son, you speak of truth. But with this battle, this morn, I must do a good act this night.

Ulric
I will walk among these men with words of fear. That will send some home! After you have gone. Take good Gifford with you, he will be a friend.

Hackett
I do not think that he will follow me, for he fears Sir Abelard greatly.

Ulric
I will make him come with you. Call him over, father.

Hackett
Good Gifford, come here and say goodbye to dear Ulric.

Gifford wakes up and comes over to Hackett.

Gifford
I have said my goodbye to your son in a prayer to our Lord.

Hackett
Say it to Ulric here. He be listening.

Hackett points up at Ulric, but Gifford cannot see him.

Gifford
Listening! This be madness. Your son be dead! I have no time to speak to a dead man, and you, sir, must be gone from here.

Hackett
Can you not see my son! *(He turns to Ulric.)* Ulric! He cannot see you.

*Gifford looks where **Ulric** is, but still cannot see him, he gives **Hackett** an odd look.*

Ulric
Do not worry, father, he will see me. Wait but a moment.

Hackett
I do wish so, Ulric, for this man thinks that I have become mad.

Gifford
I do not think this, Hackett! You be mad. I will go and fetch some food for your long journey, and then you must be gone.

***Gifford** turns his back and starts to walk away.*

Ulric
Gifford, come talk to me.

Gifford
I will speak no more with you, Hackett!

Hackett
I did not speak to you, Gifford, it was Ulric who spoke to you.

Gifford
No more of this madness! *(He turns around and looks at **Ulric**, this time seeing him.)* My god! Ulric! I have become mad like you, Hackett.

Hackett
We are not mad, Gifford! We have found help.

Gifford
It was I who carried the body of your son to this grave. This cannot be.

Ulric
Do not fear me, Gifford. I am here to help you not to hurt you.

Gifford
What help can you be? You be dead.

Ulric
You must leave this land, with Hackett, on this journey.

Gifford
I cannot leave, for if I do Sir Abelard will hunt me down.

Ulric
Do not fear Abelard. If you do not leave, you will die in battle this morn.

Hackett
You can do no good in this battle. Come with me, Gifford.

Gifford
If I do, sir, we will both die.

Ulric
If you do not take this journey and live to another dawn after this battle, I will summon the souls of the foe that die this day to haunt you until your death.

Gifford
Ghost of Ulric, do you come from above or below?

Ulric
You will learn that soon. Time for us be short. Go now and fetch food for a long journey. It be your decision if you take food for one person or two. I bid you fair well, good Gifford.

*Gifford looks towards **Ulric**, startled as he can no longer see him. However, **Ulric** remains visible to **Hackett**.*

Gifford
He be gone! Am I awake? Did I fall asleep? Am I mad?

Hackett
You are mad if you stay here and fight! Fetch the food as he has said.

Gifford
Food for a long journey, be it for one or two it be my decision. I will return soon.

Gifford leaves.

Hackett
This will be a long journey, if I am to go alone or if Gifford come with me. The road to peace be a long one for man.

Ulric
That it be, father. For many will die with this battle, and a bloody one it will be! For it will be the last battle for many a year. And crusaders will leave here broken. New wars will come and old wars will go. And for many hundreds of years birds will still fly, but man will not learn life without war. Hate and greed will still beat in the heart of many a man. Kings and leaders will still send their people out to

die and not feel a drop of sorrow for this blood they spill. They will still fight for gold, black gold. They will name these wars great wars. Foolish be the heart of man. But there be many chances to stop the killing and many men and women will try to save this race and the races of all that live upon this earth. They may do, and they may not. While birds still fly man still has brightness on his side.

Hackett
What sorrow the race of man brings to all living!

Ulric
Sorrow there will be for some! Joy there will be for some! Birds they still fly, and so a bright light still there be. Go make that light burn bright, Brave Hackett! Mourn no more for me, father, for I am joyful. Now go home and speak peace and love under your own banner. Not one of religion that causes foolish men to make war with that word. I bid you a good life . . . Fair thee well, my beloved father.

Ulric vanishes. ***Gifford*** *returns with a big bag.*

Gifford
Hackett, so still you be. Stand no more here, we must leave this land!

Hackett
As of stone am I, Gifford. I could stand, and not a movement I would make for many a day.

Gifford
Please, sir, do not do that. Let us be gone. After our long journey you will sleep, as if you are made from stone.

Hackett
I have been given a light to shine on life, and bring it to many. I may not save this world, but I will try. *(He looks at Gifford's big bag.)* Food for two, I see.

Gifford
Aye.

Hackett
I am pleased that you come with me. Let us start on our journey.

Gifford
Lets us walk swift, for we will dance for the hangman if our steps be slow ones.

Hackett pick up his belongings, while Gifford walks ahead of him.

Hackett
Swiftly we will walk Gifford.

Hackett pauses to think. Gifford looks at him.

Gifford
Hackett!

Hackett
I bid you goodbye, my son. This soil that covers your body and bones, may it grow both flowers and weeds, for room there be for both in this patch of earth.

He turns, and they quickly exit. Lights down.

Epilogue (optional)

*Spotlight up on **Eda**, centre stage.*

Eda
My beloved Ulric is gone – a child who did not see his fifteenth year. I am a mother no more. Still broken I remain, for the loss of a child is no wound that heals with one summer's sun, nor with autumn's fall, nor winter's snow. Seasons shall come and pass many times before this mother's sorrow turns to scar.

Now comes spring, and with it a bloom in me – life begins anew. I shall be mother once more. My beloved Hackett has returned to our home, burdened with tales of sorrow, his eyes storms of tears. Together we wept for our son.

He spoke bitter of the folly of war – of life that ends by the sword upon the fields of battle, soaked with man's greed from the blood of the poor. No prayer can halt the blade while man uses God as a reason for war. Victory be all the rich desire, the cost will be paid by the meek in full.

My beloved Hackett desires to take these words across this land, to give the poor hope – that they may take their sons from the jaws of rich men's battles. He be a foolish man, that would lay down his life that another mother may not endure the loss of a child in these rich men's wars.

I fear for him . . . Yet I hope, with all my soul, he shall return to me – and hold the child we are yet to meet. For a good father he was to our beloved Ulric.

Lights down.

OVER THE TOP

Rodney Quinn

When *The Lord of the Rings* movies came out, I watched the DVDs a lot. And I had this dream about three guys in a hole in the ground. They were in a trench, and they couldn't get out of it. I was thinking, 'Who are these guys? What are they doing here?' And one of them wanted to run away. Then there were bullets, and I realised it was the First World War.

When I woke up, I started to turn it into a play. I had already joined the Cork Arts Theatre, where I was working backstage. They arranged a reading for my play, and gave me good feedback. So when they held a play competition, I entered it, and won the new writers' section.

That was *Over The Top*. Although the prize was a meal at a posh restaurant in Cork, the real prize was them staging it. I didn't make the guns, but I did make the uniforms myself. And there were a lot of people who thought it was good. They liked it.

A few years later, after I'd made some changes like improving the female roles, it was performed at the South London Theatre. And in 2015, someone from Cork Arts Theatre who had moved to Australia put the play on again in Perth.

RODNEY QUINN

First Performed

First performed April 2005
Cork Arts Theatre, Cork City, Ireland

Performed March 2013
South London Theatre, London
Directed by Ben Owora and Rodney Quinn

Jack: Liam Sharkey
Tommy: Noah Wright
Witter: Theseus Stefanatos
Billy: Douglas Campbell
Sgt. Jones: Winston Forgie
William: Mark Vinson
Maggie: Kelly-Kim Cranstoun
Kate: Sue Jacobsen
Grandda: John Lyne
Mary: Robyanne Batley
Mrs Taylor: Stephanie Edwards

Characters

Jack: Late twenties, Irishman

Tommy: Late thirties, working-class Englishman

Witter: Middle-class English youth

Billy: Working-class youth

Sgt. Jones: Working-class English

William: Witter's father (middle class English)

Maggie: Tommy's wife (working-class English)

Kate: Jack's mother (Irish)

Grandda: Jack's grandfather (Irish)

Mary: Billy's girlfriend (English)

Mrs Taylor: Mary's mother (English)

OVER THE TOP

It is early winter 1918 on a battlefield in a trench somewhere in France. Early morning. There is no fighting at the moment. **Tommy** *and* **Jack** *are asleep in the trench.* **Jack**'s *back is turned to* **Tommy**. *A shot rings out in the morning sky, waking* **Tommy** *up with a start.* **Jack** *just opens his eyes.*

Tommy
What a nice dream I was having. I was in a big green meadow, there was singing and dancing, women with smiles as big as houses, men laughing and beer to fill... *(He pauses to think)* ... this trench, with joy.

Jack
Joy! Who's joy? What joy?

Tommy
Joy is another day of being alive.

Jack
Another day to die.

Tommy
Come on Jack, it will soon be over, be a week, hey a fortnight and back home. The Germans are on the run. Peace is near.

***Jack** picks up an empty cup, looking at **Tommy**.*

Jack
War is the cup, peace is the water, these lips are dry, but I have no water to wet them, but I have an empty cup, which will never hold water again. I could fill it with blood, for there is plenty flowing around here.

Tommy looks at Jack like he is going a little mad.

Tommy
Jack, we'll make it. Stay strong lad.

Jack
We run, we run, get us out of this war alive, we go to Spain.

Tommy
Are you going mad?

Jack
Mad is this hell we live day by day.

Tommy
That it is lad.

There is a brief silence.

Jack
Do you think, Tommy, that this circle of hate will even end?

Tommy
This war will soon end, Jack lad, but it wouldn't shock me to see another great war happen before we grow old . . . Because lessons haven't been learned here.

Jack
You're right, Tommy. It's the same old mistakes from day to day, year to year.

Tommy
Let's hope that we're too old to fight in that one.

Jack
I don't think I'll get the chance to grow old if I leave my life in the hands of these people giving the orders around here.

Tommy
Keep your head down Jack, and with a bit of luck the Germans shooting at us couldn't shoot a turkey a foot away.

*Sgt. Jones enters with **Witter** and **Billy**. **Billy** is carrying a pot with porridge, **Witter** is carrying a teapot.*

Sgt. Jones
Morning lads!

Tommy *(Very bright and happy)*
Morning Sergeant!

Jack *(Like he could not care)*
Morning.

*Sgt. Jones looks at **Witter** and **Billy** who are standing still, and makes a gesture to them to hurry up.*

Sgt. Jones
Well boys, feed the men! They can't fight on empty bellies.

Tommy *and **Jack** have their hands out with a bowl in one and a cup in the other. **Witter** and **Billy** fill them up. **Tommy** and **Jack** look at the food with grimaces on their faces. Watery porridge and weak tea is what they are given. They thank the lads in a 'thanks-for-nothing' way.*

Tommy
   Ta.

Jack
   Gee, thanks, lovely!

Tommy
   There's water in your cup now, Jack.

Jack
   There's water in my bowl too.

Sgt. Jones
   Only the best for our boys. You wouldn't get better on Oxford Street; there's a war on you know.

Jack *(Sarcastically)*
   Yes, in Oxford Street. Can I be sent there to help them fight?

Sgt. Jones
   Very funny lad.

Tommy
   That's our Jack, good old Irish humour.

Sgt. Jones *turns and talks to **Witter** and **Billy***

Sgt. Jones
Lads, put that food away and get back here with your rifles and equipment! You are to accompany these two comedians.

Witter and Billy go off left with the food

Sgt. Jones
Men, take these two lads under your wings!

Jack
When we get over the top, I'm not carrying them. I'll tell you that for nothing.

Tommy
Jack! We'll take care of them, Sergeant.

Sgt. Jones
God knows how old they are, they came last night... I think their guns are older than them. Private Blair, quiet lad, looks more frightened than I've ever seen.

Tommy
Do you know when we go over the top, Sergeant?

Sgt. Jones
Order will be given around 11 o'clock. I hear it will be a walk in the park. On their last legs those Germans.

Jack
How do they know that?

Sgt. Jones
Those boys in the air, that's how.

Tommy
A walk, you say.

Sgt. Jones
Yes, but I would take your gun just in case.

Witter and Billy come back with their rifles and their gear.

Sgt. Jones
OK, privates, I will be back later.

Sgt. Jones walks off. Billy sits down. Witter stands up straight and proud to talk to the lads.

Witter
Hello there, chaps, my name is Witter. Isn't it a lovely day? The sun is shining and there's a clear blue sky.

Jack
Sit down, you stupid twit, before you get shot.

Witter goes over to Tommy.

Witter
And hello to you my friend.

Tommy
Hello Witter, Billy; my name is Tommy. This unhappy soul is Jack. Don't you worry about him. For some mad reason he would rather be somewhere else. Don't know why, for the life of me.

Jack
We're in a big damn hole, with rats eating our food, half

the German army trying to kill us, and breakfast is watery porridge. Yes, it's a lovely day; yes, it's a lovely jolly day.

Witter
Well it is a lovely day; what more could we ask for?

Jack
I couldn't give a damn what the weather is like; I'd just like to be alive come night. Oh, and just a small thing . . . Not to be here and waiting to die.

Witter
So you would like the heavens to open up and soak us to the skin?

Jack
What damn difference does it make? You fool!

Witter
Some people are never happy.

Tommy
Lads! Yes, it's a damn fine day and we all would love nothing better than to be sitting on grass, sipping a nice pint of beer, back with our loved ones . . . But we are in a hell hole of a field covered in mud waiting to kill or be killed . . . this is our lot, so let's keep our anger for the battle to come. Now, let's enjoy this lovely, watery porridge!

Billy
Sorry about that porridge, I made it.

*Jack is not listening to **Billy**. He looks at **Tommy**.*

Jack
Look around at all these young men ... No, boys! Just waiting to die. What a waste of life, and for what?

Tommy
For their land, for their families, maybe for their King.

Jack
Damn their King! He would not die for them nor would his family. And for Britain? I will say no more!

Witter
Hey now, be good and kind when you speak of my great and wise King and country.

Jack
Great? What is so great about him? If he was so great and wise, why then could he not stop this mindless slaughter? You know why! It's power! He feels bloody great knowing all these poor fools are dying in his name.

Billy
We are toys for their games.

Witter
We are fighting for him so he can keep all that's great about our land, and stop those nasty Germans coming over and making us speak French. (*He gives a little laugh.*)

Jack
If you don't shut up, I will hit you, Witter the twitter!

***Billy** looks at **Witter**.*

Billy
   Twitter, ha!

Tommy
   Lads! (*He moves his hands in a way for them all to calm down.*) How did you get that name 'Witter', Witter?

Witter
   My father said when I was born I looked like a warrior, a wise warrior.

Jack
   Tommy, stop me, I will hit him. I'll let you in on a secret; you're not wise! And as for being a warrior – yes, I can just see you winning the war all on your own. Witter the warrior!

Witter
   That's what it means, wise warrior. It's a Teutonic name. But I think my father was having a laugh.

Tommy
   Having a laugh?

Witter
   My surname is Witmarsh. Witter Witmarsh. Sounds a bit odd, don't you think?

Jack
   Teutonic, you said?

Witter
   Yes.

Jack
That's German.

Billy
Old German, I think.

Witter
I don't know, it's just a name after all.

Jack
You sure you're not fighting for the wrong country?

Tommy
Jack, stop it! You got family yourself, Witter?

Jack
You got a girl, Vitter?

Witter
No, I got a dog.

Tommy, Jack and Billy give Witter an odd look.

Billy
A dog?

Tommy
A girl would be better. You can talk to them, lad.

Witter
I talk to my dog!

Billy
Does it talk back?

Witter
Now don't be a silly billy, Billy.

Jack
What do you say to it? Give me a kiss, doggy, and I'll give you a nice big bone?

Witter
You may kiss dogs, Jack. I do not!

Jack
You know that hitting him idea? It's not gone away, Tommy.

Tommy
Save it for the Germans Jack.

Jack
I'll try.

Billy
What about your family Witter?

Witter
What about them?

Jack
Have you any still alive, he's asking you! Fool!

Witter
Yes.

Billy
Who?

Tommy
Tell us lad?

Witter
My Papa is still alive.

Jack
You mean your Da!

Jack gets up and starts to walk away.

Witter
Da?

Jack
Your father. (*Shouting at him, he goes off stage, and shouts back.*) Mr Bloody Witmarsh! You cabbage!

Tommy
Don't mind him, lad.

Billy
Did he make you join the army?

Witter
No, I signed up when I came of age.

Tommy
Why didn't you sign before you came of age, if you were so eager to join up?

Witter
I tried when I turned seventeen, but they told me to come back when I turned fifteen.

Tommy
You do look young, lad.

Billy
Was your father happy with you joining the army?

Witter
No!

Tommy
What did he say when you told him?

Witter
I got up very early on my birthday, so I could go to the army office and sign up and get back in time for me and Papa to walk to work together. But Papa also got up early.

Billy
So did he find out what you were going to do?

Witter
No. He came into the dining room, with a big smile on his face.

Lights dim. **William** *walks in holding a small box.* **Tommy** *and* **Billy***'s heads are down with their eyes closed.*

Witter
Good morning, Papa.

Lights up. **Witter** *stands up and walks to* **William***.*

William
> Good morning, son. I must say you are awake very early this morning.

Witter
> I have a lot of jobs to do today, Papa.

William
> Not enough to get you up this early, son.

Witter
> I better go now, Papa.

William
> Wait a moment there, young Mr Witmarsh, Can a father not give his only son his best wishes on his happy birthday?

Witter
> Yes, you can Papa.

William
> Happy eighteenth birthday, Witter.

*He goes to give the box to **Witter**.*

Witter
> I must go, Papa. I will be back before you go to work.

William
> Witter!

***Witter** turn his back and moves away. **William** walks off.*

Lights up. **Jack** *walks on.*

Billy
What does your father do for a living, Witter?

Witter
My father owns the Witmarsh family store.

Tommy
Where is that, Witter?

Witter
East London.

Jack
Bet he didn't let you run it, Vitter?

***Witter** looks at **Jack** in angry silence.*

Tommy
So did you take your father's gift, lad?

Witter
Not then. I had to get to the army office.

Jack
What gift did Papa Witmarsh get you, then?

Tommy
Did you find out?

Witter
Yes!

Billy
Tell us, then. And what he said when he found out that you joined up.

Jack
Yes there, Vitter. What did Papa Vitmarsh say?

Tommy
What is your Father's name, Witter?

Jack
I know, Tommy . . . It's Mitter, or maybe . . . Fitter, Sitter or could be even Litter!

Witter
William.

Jack
William Witmarsh!? They like their Ws in your family. What was your Mother? Wictori?

Witter
No!

Tommy
So, Witter, what did your Father say?

Billy
And what was his birthday present to you?

Witter
I got back home as my Papa was about to leave for work . . .

Lights dim. **Tommy**, **Jack** *and* **Billy**'s *heads are down with their eyes closed.*

William *(From off stage)*
  Witter!

William *walks in. Lights on him.* **Witter** *stands up and walks to* **William**.

Witter
  Yes Father.

William *pulls out his pocket watch on a chain.*

William
  Look at the time, Witter.

Witter
  I don't have a watch, Father.

William
  Well it's a about time you had a watch.

Witter
  I do not need one Father.

William
  You are late again, and now I am also late. We should have been in the store by now, young man, so I think it is time that you had a good time piece.

Witter
  I will not use it, Father.

William
You will! *(He takes a small black box out of his pocket and hands it to **Witter**.)* Happy birthday, son.

***Witter** opens the box and closes it again.*

Witter
I have no use for a gold watch, Father, where I am going.

William
What do you mean . . . ? Where you are going?

Witter
I'm leaving home.

William
Leaving home? . . . Where are you going?

Witter
France, I think. I joined the army this morning.

William
What a fool of a son I have! I should have known you would enlist when you came of age.

Witter
I would be a fool to waste my life working my days until I am old and grey with you shouting at me. While the world is having this great adventure, I must . . .

William
Shouting at you? I am teaching you, and I am trying to stop you daydreaming your life away . . . So you think that you're wasting your life working for your father? I have

given you everything a young man could need and wish for.

Witter
I am bored working in your store . . . I want an adventure! I never want to work for you again. I am going to have an adventure and live a full life and not one of boredom, stacking shelves every day in a dusty old shop.

William
I have heard that word adventure before from many a young man. Now almost every day I sell flowers to their mothers, for them to kneel and cry over their fallen sons' graves. And for the mothers that have no graves to cry over, they buy flowers on their beloved's birthday and do their sombre weeping in the church. Memories are all they have from their child's desire for an adventure. This kind of adventure may have the same outcome for you, Witter, but you will have no mother to cry over your grave and no father.

Witter
I must leave now, Father.

William
You go on your adventure, Witter, and if God spares your life from this mindless slaughter, do not return to this house, for I no longer have a son.

William turn his back walks off.

Witter
Goodbye.

Witter *sits down. Lights up.* ***Jack*** *walks on.*

Tommy
You broke your father's heart, lad.

Witter
I've been working in that store since I was twelve on a wage no better than a newspaper boy.

Tommy
You got board and lodging for free for eighteen years.

Witter
I paid that off with six years as a badly paid shop boy. But now I'm free from that hell.

Jack
I would gladly work for your da for a cup of tea and a scone a day if I could get out of this hell.

Witter
Hell! This is no hell, this is freedom!

Jack
Fool! Give it a day and the word hell will be your only word!

Billy
Did you keep the watch your father give you Witter?

Witter
Yes.

Billy
Have you got it here?

Witter
Yes

Witter takes the watch out of his pocket.

Tommy
You still must miss your father if you kept the watch . . . ?

Witter holds the watch up for them to see it.

Witter
I brought it with me by mistake.

Jack gets up and goes to Witter.

Jack
And by mistake put it into your army-issued tunic. *(Jack grabs the watch from Witter.)* Let me take a closer look.

Witter
Hey!

Tommy
Jack! Give it back to the lad!

Jack has a good look at the watch.

Jack
Worth a bob or two this.

Witter
Give it back!

Jack holds the watch up.

Jack
I'll make a deal with you. You give me this watch, which in a way means years of boredom to you, and I will let you have the freedom of doing my latrine-digging duties for the next two weeks . . . If you live that long. *(**Jack** swings the watch.)* Tick tock, tick tock, we all fall down.

***Witter** gets up and goes over to **Jack**.*

Witter
No thank you!

***Jack** hands the watch back to **Witter**.*

Jack
My last offer then . . . until you die! Which might just be a few hours.

Tommy
Jack, let us have bit of peace now!

*The four of them sit in silence and some of them check their rifles, until **Jack** starts humming 'It's a Long Way to Tipperary'.*

Tommy
Who have you left at home, Billy?

Billy
I'm sixth of eight children in my family.

Tommy
Eight children. That's a big family!

Jack
Billy, you got a girl, or maybe you got a cat?

Witter gives Jack a dirty look. Jack gives him a big smile back.

Billy
We do have a cat at home. I had a girl before I joined up.

Tommy
You finish it then?

Billy
No! Her name is Mary. We've been courting for two months. She made me join up.

Jack
Sounds like love. She made you join the army.

Tommy
How lad?

Billy
One Friday I was waiting in the park . . . we meet every Friday after work for a . . . chat.

Jack
We know what you mean, boy. You had a bit of 'decent chat'!

Tommy
Jack! Go on, lad.

Billy
She turns up late and crying and . . .

Lights dim. **Mary** *walks in crying.* **Tommy, Jack** *and* **Witter**'s *heads are down with their eyes closed.*

Billy
I'm all a worry and all.

Billy *stands up and walks to* **Mary**.

Billy
I say, Mary, what's the matter, love?

Mary
It's my brother John.

Billy
He's dead Mary, love.

Mary
A year today. My mother has gone to church to pray and weep for him.

Billy
It will take her many years. There is many a family that will need time to recover from this war.

Mary
Your mother doesn't cry?

Billy
She has lost a few nephews.

Mary
But no sons.

Billy
She has no sons old enough but me.

Mary
Is she not ashamed?

Billy
Why would she be?

Mary
Most mothers around here have sons that are out there fighting, or they have lost sons out there.

Billy
She does not want me to join the army.

Mary
You must tell her that it is your duty. And if you don't, Billy, I can't see you anymore.

Billy
Mary, love . . .

Mary
They all think that you're a coward.

Billy
Who?

Mary
All down the factory . . . and my father and mother.

Billy
What do they know about war?

Mary
They know that you can't hide from your duty.

Billy
So they want me to die too.

Mary
I think they're right, Billy. Why don't you want to join the army?

Billy
I don't want to fight. Enough have died.

Mary
See, you are a coward Billy!

Billy
I'm not, don't say that . . .

Mary
I can't be seen with a coward.

Billy
I'm not, Mary. I love you.

Mary
I don't love cowards. I got a letter from Duncan Smith, my old boyfriend. He is fighting like a hero in France. He said he still loves me.

Billy
He also loved Rita Colman, remember her?

Mary

He's sorry for that. It was a mistake. Anyway, he's a man, not a coward like you.

Billy

I told you, I'm no coward. I'll show you.

Mary

Join up, Billy. I'll show you a time tonight.

Billy

Will you still be my girl if I join, Mary?

Mary

Yes, Billy. I will. I'll even go to the dock and wave you off.

Billy

Will you still be here for me when I get back?

Mary

Yes. Come on, now. You go down to the army office. I'll go home and wait for you. See you back at the house later.

Billy

Alright, love.

Mary

Bye, love, see you later then.

Mary kisses Billy on the cheek and runs off skipping and smiling. Billy stands looking out.

Billy
I went to the army office to sign up and then I went home to tell my Mother . . . She was not happy with me.

Witter
Did Mary show you a good time later?

Jack
What would you know about that, dogman?

Tommy
So was Mary happy you joined up, lad?

Billy
I turned up at Mary's house. As I was going up to the door, her mother came out.

Mrs Taylor enters looking like she has been crying.

Mrs Taylor
Hello, Billy love.

Billy
Hello, Mrs Taylor.

Mrs Taylor
Sorry, Billy, I'm not my best today. It's our John's anniversary, and I'm feeling a bit sad.

Billy
Mary told me earlier. Wish I had met your John, Mrs Taylor.

Mrs Taylor
He was lovely lad ... But please, Billy, don't get me crying again. How are you, love?

Billy
Could be better. I've come to see Mary?

Mrs Taylor
She's not here, love. She's gone down to Ann Smith's house, to help her prepare her brother's room.

Billy
Duncan coming home?

Mrs Taylor
Yes, he's coming out of hospital tomorrow.

Billy
I didn't know that he was back in England.

Mrs Taylor
He's back a long while now. Mary and Ann been going along to see him for the last two weeks.

Billy
Mary's been saying that he's fighting like a hero in France.

Mrs Taylor
Hero? He shot himself in the foot, and the wound turned septic ... The conditions in those trenches are not the cleanest, so I've heard ... He was lucky that he didn't lose his foot, or even his leg, thank God.

Billy
He's still a hero to Ann and Mary.

Mrs Taylor
You may be right there, Billy, but I don't like that lad all that much, I must say, he's a bit of a fool. Well he must be to go and shoot himself in the foot now, mustn't he?

Billy
He must be . . . I better go now. Will you tell Mary that I dropped by. And that I'll be leaving tomorrow.

Mrs Taylor
Where are you going, love?

Billy
The army.

Mrs Taylor
No, Billy, you foolish thing! Only yesterday, myself and Mr Taylor were telling Mary to make sure that boy doesn't do a silly thing and join up to get himself killed!

Billy looks a little lost.

Billy
She did try to stop me, but it's my duty to fight for my country.

Mrs Taylor
Too many boys have died . . .

She stops to think and breaks down crying.

Billy
Please don't get upset, Mrs Taylor.

Mrs Taylor
I'm all right, Billy love . . . Here she is now.

Mary
Hello, Billy.

Mrs Taylor
Mary! Billy here has been telling me that he joined up to fight.

Mary
That's great, when are you leaving?

Mrs Taylor
It is not great, Mary! Didn't me and your father tell you to make sure that he didn't join the army?

Mary
Yes, Mam, but it is his duty to King and country.

Billy
It is my duty.

Mrs Taylor
The young men of this county have paid their duty to the King.

Mary
People will think that he is a coward if he doesn't go and fight.

Mrs Taylor
I would be happier for my son to be a living coward than a dead solider!

Mary
John was no coward, he joined up as soon as war broke out, like most men.

Billy
I was too young.

Mrs Taylor
And you still are, Billy love. In over three years of war, and many dead, you learn that maybe we have given too much.

Mary
When do you sail, Billy love?

Billy
Don't know, Mary, but I have to report to the barracks by four o'clock tomorrow.

Mrs Taylor
Let us hope that the war has ended by the time you have to leave us, Billy. I'm tired of crying for loved ones . . . I'm going to church again to say one last prayer to my John . . . *(She starts to cry.)* I'll pray that God brings you back to us safe, Billy . . . Look after yourself and don't be a hero and go shoot yourself in the foot now.

She smiles, but then she start to cry. ***Mrs Taylor*** *walks off.*

Billy
You lied to me, Mary.

Mary
I didn't want to be seen with a coward... But you're not, Billy! You're off to fight, are you excited?

Billy
No!

Mary
I'm excited for you, Billy. I'll miss you.

Billy
Will you?

Mary
Yes.

Billy
What about that good time you were going to show me?

Mary
I can't tonight. Maybe before you leave.

Billy
Why not tonight?

Mary
I'm going to see Duncan in hospital... He's just a friend now. It's you I love, Billy.

Billy
Do you, Mary?

Mary
Yes, I do. I've got to go now. Meet you tomorrow at noon

in the park, love. *(She kisses him on the check.)* Goodbye, Billy.

Billy looks at Mary as she happily walks off.

Billy
Goodbye, Mary.

Billy sits back down. Lights up.

Jack
Odd girl that, Mary.

Billy
That, and more.

Tommy
That she is, lad. She didn't take after her mother

Billy
No, she didn't.

Tommy
She seems like a good woman, that Mrs Taylor ... Did you see Mary then next day, then?

Billy
I never saw Mary again ... She never seemed to be home when I dropped by.

Witter
Very odd girl. So, she never showed you that good time, then?

Jack
Shut up, you fool.

Tommy
Yes, Witter, do that.

The four of them check their rifles in silence, **Billy** *with head down.*

Billy
You got a girl, Tommy?

Tommy
I have a girl, well a wife. I must say twenty years we've been together but she's still my girl. Maggie, she was sixteen when I met her. I was seventeen. We got four youngens – George, James, Emily, and wee baby Johnny.

Witter
My dog is called Johnny . . . I miss him so much.

Jack
Tommy, let me hit him just the once!

Tommy
Calm it, Jack.

Jack
It's starting to become a hard thing to do, I must say.

Tommy
I miss my Maggie. One good woman! Hard worker. No one sits around when Maggie's got work to do! You gotta help! Even me, on my only day off! Believe that.

Witter
A man needs a rest day.

Tommy
I would try, but she would come out and give me jobs to do! I can just see her now saying things like . . .

Lights dim. **Maggie** *walks on stage right talking like she is in her own home.* **Tommy** *is looking at her.* **Jack**, **Witter** *and* **Billy**'s *heads are down with their eyes closed. She talks in a slightly cross way.*

Maggie
Come now, Tommy. You'd be showing the youngens bad habits. Get up off the ground and go down to Lewis's farm an' bring us some eggs and milk. Oh, yes, on yer way down, drop some of that cake to Lizzie Price. Don't eat any either. See if her young one's over the fever. Send them my love and tell her I'll pop by soon. I'm so busy right now

Tommy
I will, Maggie love.

Maggie
There is never enough time in a day to do a mother's job.

Tommy
And there is never enough time to do a wife job?

Maggie
Now what is a wife's job, Tommy Crompton?

Tommy *stands up and walks towards her.*

Tommy
Many things.

Maggie
I have no time for your many things, Tommy. I'm too busy bringing up our little things.

Tommy
Would be good, love, if we could have a day all to ourselves, like that time we went down to the coast and swam for ages and then we had fun in the sand dunes.

Maggie
Will you stop now, Tommy. That was years ago . . . and as I remember you feel asleep.

Tommy
Did I? . . . Yes, I did.

Maggie
Making ends meet is the only thing we have time for these days, we're father and mother now! Husband and wife we are too, but this is second, for the youngens are first. I do wish someday that we could have time and money for us again, Tommy.

Tommy
Me too, Maggie love.

Maggie
They were good days, and when this war is over maybe life won't be so hard and we might find time for your many things, Tommy Crompton . . . Now get yourself off down to Lizzie Price with you.

Tommy
I'm halfway there, Maggie.

***Tommy** turns around and sits back down.*

Maggie
Hurry back now, love.

***Maggie** walks off stalking. **Tommy** smiles but is a bit sad. Lights up.*

Jack
She sounds like my Ma. Hard, but a good heart.

Tommy
That she is. But the day I was called up for the army, she was not hard.

*Lights dim. **Maggie** walks on stage right talking with a letter in her hand and hands it to **Tommy**, who stands up and walks towards her.*

Maggie
Tommy, there's a letter for you. Please tell me it's not what I think it is . . . open it and please tell me so . . . Please!

Tommy
It is what you think it is, dear.

Maggie
No, no Tommy, why you? I need you. We need you.

Tommy
I'll come home. I will, love.

Maggie
Remember all those men we used to know. Down in village most are dead now. It's a death sentence, Tommy.

Tommy
I got to go, Maggie. I got to do it. It's my duty. *(He holds Maggie for a short while.)* We better find the time for those 'many things' before I go, love.

Maggie
Will we go down to the coast, one last time Tommy?

He steps away from her.

Tommy
It won't be our last time. We'll go many times when this war is all over, love.

Maggie
I hope so, Tommy.

***Maggie** walks off right very upset. **Tommy** looks sad. Lights up.*

Billy
She's got a good heart within her, your Maggie.

Witter
My dog's got a good heart. Sometimes he . . .

Tommy *(Looking at **Witter**, shaking his head)*
Witter, Witter. Come on tell us about your loved ones, Jack.

Jack

All right, then. But I'll hit you, boy, if you say you have a dog named after any of my family.

Witter

I've got only one dog now, but I did have another called Rover. Would that be the name of any in your family, Jack?

Jack

Boy, you'll be rovering close to those Germans very soon with a boot up the behind, if you say anything bad about my family, sonny. Watch your lip!

Tommy

Come on, Jack, tell us about them then.

Jack

Still got my Ma, and Grandda, My Father died when I was a wee lad. They're farmers. Had an older brother. He got killed in France, in the early days of the war. I joined up after his death. They were not happy with him joining the British army.

Tommy

I'd say they were not happy with you doing such a thing after your brother's death.

Jack

You can be sure they were not. There were tears from Mother and loud words from both. That was the last time I saw them. That sad day will only die in my mind the day I die.

Tommy
What were those loud words they spoke at you?

Jack
I was walking out of the house, and my mother was in the yard.

Tommy, Witter and Billy's heads go down. Jack is looking up. Lights dim. His mother, Kate, enters.

Kate
Where are you going, Jack?

Jack
I'm going to England, Ma.

Kate
Why, Jack?

Jack
To join the British army.

Kate
How could you! It's only a fortnight since we heard of Michael's parting, may the lord have mercy on his soul.

She crosses herself.

Jack
I know, Ma.

Kate
Am I to lose another son?

Jack
I wish not, Ma.

Kate
War is not for the living, Jack.

Jack
I must go, Ma. I will miss the train.

Kate
What kind of goodbye is this to your mother, Jack?

Jack
An easy one, with less pain, Ma.

Kate
When you walk out on us, do you think I will not feel hurt?

Jack
You will, Ma, and so will I.

Kate
Are you not going to say goodbye to your Grandda? . . . Da, come out here!

Grandda enters.

Grandda
What is it, Kate? Has someone died?

Kate
As good as, Da.

Grandda
Are you going somewhere, Jack?

Kate
He's off to England, Da... to fight for the British... and our Michael's not a month passed away... *(She crosses herself.)* ... may the Lord have mercy on his soul.

Grandda
Will you let the boy speak, Kate. Is this, true Jack?

Jack
Yes, Grandda.

Grandda
Am I to have another grandson who dies for the British?

Kate
How will we run the farm without sons?!

Grandda
We need you here. This farm is all we've got, and without you we mightn't be able to it run it.

Kate
We could end up in the poor house if we lose the farm.

Grandda
Could you not stay a month until we find someone to help?

Kate
Please, Jack.

Jack

There are enough farm people in the county that would be glad to work here, Grandda.

Grandda

There is, Jack. But they're not my only grandson.

Kate

Da, get him to change his mind!

Grandda

Don't think we can, Kate.

Kate

He must, Da. I can't lose another son.

Grandda

Son, why not fight against the English rather than with them?

Kate

It's not our war. We got our own war. The Germans are not our enemy, son. Don't be foolish.

Jack

They will be.

Grandda

Look at it this way, son, the Germans are fighting the English and so are we!

Kate

Don't join this damn war.

Jack
I must do this for Michael and for me.

Kate
Michael wouldn't want you do a foolish thing.

Jack
He didn't think it was foolish.

Grandda
Leave the boy now, Kate. Would you not get the morning train, Jack?

Jack
I must go now.

Grandda
There will be no shame if you come back in few days.

Kate
We won't tell anybody where you have gone. If you see any one on the road, Jack, just tell them that you're off to Dublin.

Grandda
We don't want you to leave, but I must part with you as your loving granddad. Goodbye Jack and take of yourself.

Kate
Come back to us, Jack. I'll say a prayer to St Christopher to keep you safe, every night, son.

She hugs him.

Jack
Bye, Ma. Bye Grandda.

Jack turns around and walks away from them, then stops.

Kate *(Shouting)*
Take care of yourself in Dublin, Jack.

***Grandda** and **Kate** exit. Lights up.*

Jack
I turned away and walked back up the path. I didn't look back.

Billy
Must have been hard. Why did you join up?

Jack
To kill my brother's killer.

Witter
There are so many Germans out there, how are you going to know who it is? He may already be dead.

Tommy
Be quiet there, Witter, lad.

Jack
In a way, my Grandda was right. The Germans and us are both fighting the British, but for different reasons.

Tommy
What reasons?

Jack
The Irish are fighting for Ireland; the Germans are fighting to take over the whole damn lot.

Tommy
I see what you mean.

Jack
I think if the Germans took Britain they would not stop there, and we in Ireland would no longer be fighting the British, but the Germans!

Tommy
You could be right there, Jack.

Jack
I'm tired of seeing all this death in the name of Britain and this damn army.

Witter
Why? The British army is a great army and Britain is a great land.

Jack
Have you been locked in a wardrobe for the best part of your life, boy?

Billy
Jack is Irish, Witter.

Witter
Same thing, they just talk funny.

Jack
If we get through this fun time we are going to have with the Germans trying to kill us, then I will kill you. So you better hope I do not make it.

Tommy
The Irish have been fighting us – well the British army – for many years for their independence. So a lot of people in Ireland would look on Jack and others fighting for British as a . . .

Jack
As a traitor

Witter
Britain will not look on you as a traitor, but as a hero.

Jack
What is so great about Britain, where most of the people are slaves to the rich, where they have to work all their God given days to keep a roof over their heads and food on the table for them and their family! What life is that?

Tommy
Sometimes I can see why war is good to some men, a change of life, no children, and a different job to do . . .

Jack
Not too sure about children not being around. Hey Witter, hey Billy!

Witter
I have no children. I'm too young for them.

Jack
Yes, you are. You could nearly say that you still are one. But not in an hour. In an hour you will die like a man, and that's what you will do, child.

Tommy
But don't forget, Jack, he's got Johnny, the dog, waiting for him. Yes, Johnny, same name as my wee lad.

Witter
I don't want to die.

Tommy
Well, we know some day we must. At thirty-seven, I must be the oldest in this trench,

Billy
I'd say you are, Tommy. Maybe Sarge could be a bit older than you.

Tommy
If we could go over the top now and look at some of those dead bodies, we'd be looking at boys. Most of them no older than eighteen years, some as young as sixteen. Maybe some even younger. What a waste.

Witter
I don't want to grow old either.

*Tommy looks quizzically at **Witter** and nods his head.*

Tommy
... Cake and eat it boy. I want to grow old with my Maggie and the youngens.

Jack
We don't have to die here.

Tommy
What do you mean, Jack.

Jack
Over that hill to our near right is a thick wood and beyond the wood is an old farmhouse and beside it more woods, then a road, the road south and Spain.

Tommy
You make it sound like we would be going down to the beach for a swim. As easy as that, hey Jack.

Billy
It's a little mad.

Tommy
It is, boy, but it's all a bit mad here.

Witter
Do you mean desert?

Jack
No, I mean bread and butter pudding! . . . To get the hell out, and not die here.

Tommy
Jack, I don't know, they could catch us, and then shoot us.

Jack
We are going to die anyway.

Tommy
If we did get away, I'd never be able to see my family again. I could never go back to home.

Witter
Your family would hate you for not being dead.

Jack
Hate me for not being dead?

Witter
Their memory of you. To them you died a hero. You died with honour for your king and country.

Tommy
Yes, Jack, you come back say a year after the war, and tell them you ran and that you were hiding in Spain for years. How would they take it?

Witter
'Coward!' they would say.

Jack
I could live with that, because I am no coward. You know that Tommy.

Tommy
I know, Jack, you're no coward, but neither am I.

Billy (*Speaking to himself*)
Nor I.

Witter
Does not sound like that to me.

Jack
This is not my fight, not my cause. Maybe I'll go back and fight a fight worth fighting for, if you can say any war is worth a drop of anybody's blood.

Tommy
I know, Jack, this is not your war, and if you went home and fought for something you believed in, I would not hate you for it.

Witter
I would.

Billy
It does not pain me if you make your own way, Jack.

Tommy
I did not start this war, and I believe it is a sad waste of good men and boys. But for right or wrong I am here, and if I must I will die here, not for us, not for any other member of this bloody army, but for my wife and four children, for any freedom it makes for them.

Billy
I too will do my duty for right or wrong.

Jack
I'm tired of this fighting and of this war. I cannot feel that any war is worth fighting, not even the one in my own land. But it is a fight for people, for the poor. It is not about greed, it's about dignity, about feeding your family.

Witter
I haven't got a family anymore.

Jack

British people, and for that matter the German people, their fight should not be against each other. Their battle should be against those that keep them down. A fight against those who send them into this bloody mindless war.

Tommy

If you get out of this hell, will you carry on the fight?

Jack

My brother's death, this army, this war, the war at home, has made me what I am. If I go home I might be shot as a traitor. If I go to England, the same. I may hate again. I may even have to kill again, but only to keep my freedom.

Billy

This war will change us all, and not for the better.

Sgt. Jones enters. He is carrying a tin with rum in it.

Sgt. Jones

Come get your rum.

Witter

Rum, I'll get some for us.

Sgt. Jones

Get one bottle for you four, Private Witmarsh.

Billy

Will we soon be fighting, Sergeant?

Sgt. Jones
Have a good drink, lad, soon I will give the orders . . . be brave, son.

Billy
You got any family at home, Sergeant?

Sgt. Jones
No, they're all gone, son.

Tommy
Did you ever marry, Sergeant?

Sgt. Jones
Yes, I did.

Billy
Where is your wife now?

Sgt. Jones *(Pointing up)*
She's up there with our child and our Lord is looking after them.

Tommy
What happened, Sergeant?

Sgt. Jones
She died in child birth . . . Fifteen years ago now. A short while after her death, I married myself to the Army.

Jack
Has it been a good marriage?

Sgt. Jones
Like many a marriage it's good until the fighting starts. Now I'd like a divorce.

They all laugh.

Sgt. Jones
I'll be back in a while, lads.

***Sgt. Jones** goes off.*

Jack
Come with me, Tommy.

Tommy
I can't, Jack. This is my lot here. I have to stay.

Jack
Billy, will you come with me?

Billy
I would like to, to get out of this, but back home I think I'm looked at already as a coward. I'll try to get home a living hero.

***Witter** comes back with two bottles. He gives one to **Tommy** and the other he opens and drinks some. **Billy** takes the bottle off him and takes a big gulp.*

Witter
Here, Tommy.

Tommy
Won't be long now. Be catching those bullets soon.

Witter
How do you know?

Tommy
The free drink. We get it when we're about to go over the top . . . and the Sergeant told me.

He smiles.

Jack
Here's to freedom!

Tommy
Here's to the family!

Billy
Yes, to my family and an old girlfriend!

Witter
Here's to England, St George and the King, and that we all go out honourable heroes!

***Tommy** and **Jack** shake their heads, **Billy** just smiles, and all give **Witter** an odd look. **Jack** takes the bottle off **Tommy**, pours a drink in all four cups.*

Jack
Here's to Spain.

Billy
Yes, to sunny Spain, Jack.

Tommy
I hope you make it

Witter
Cowards! I'll make sure your families get a white feather for you.

Jack hits Witter across the face with his rum bottle, knocking him out. Billy and Tommy look at Witter falling.

Jack
Here's to Witter, the warrior, or otherwise known as Sir Witter the twitter!

Billy goes to see if Witter is OK.

Billy
He'll be out for a while.

Sgt. Jones comes in and calls out.

Sgt. Jones
Troops, we go over the top in five minutes. We'll be pushing onto the Germans' front line.

Tommy
Jack, you may have saved his life.

Jack
Dear me, what a mistake. *(He laughs.)* I do hope the boy lives and learns from this war. I would not have hurt him anymore than that.

Tommy
Good luck. Here, Jack, take this letter. If you make it, look me up, or look up my family. It's my address. Tell them I love them and I missed them.

Jack
I will, Tommy. Keep yourself alive as long as you can.

Tommy
I'll try. *(Turns to **Billy**.)* Billy, lad, stay close.

***Sgt. Jones** comes in and calls out.*

Sgt. Jones
Charge, for King and country and St George.

***Witter** comes to. He looks at **Jack** saying goodbye to **Tommy**. He stands up, gets his gun and shouts.*

Witter
TRAITOR!

***Billy** tries to stop **Witter**. **Witter** stabs his bayonet into **Jack**'s back. He slides to the ground, dying. **Tommy** hits **Witter** with the butt of his rifle, knocking him out.*

Tommy
Witter, why?

Jack
Well, no Spain for me, Tommy.

***Jack** dies. **Billy** has been hit with fear.*

Tommy
Spain sounds good right now, Jack, but I can't. I got to be a murderer again and kill in the name of our so-called great King, or maybe die in that name.

*Tommy pours the rest of the rum on **Witter**.*

Tommy
Here's to Jack, boy. Here's to life, and may you learn all about it, son. Come, Billy lad, stay near now.

***Tommy** and **Billy** take their guns and go over the top.*

Tommy
King and country!

End.

www.ingramcontent.com/pod-product-compliance
Lightning Source LLC
Chambersburg PA
CBHW030306100526
44590CB00012B/534